Lavender is a Boring Color

LAVENDER IS A BORING COLOR

Copyright © 2023 by Kevin Black. All rights reserved. No part of this publication may be stored in a retrieval system, scanned, downloaded, used, or reproduced in any manner whatsoever without prior written permission—except in the case of brief quotations in the context of published reviews. Piracy of copyrighted materials is a criminal offense.

This title is also available in e-book format.

Satin Colorway Publishing,
Los Angeles, CA 90068

www.satincolorway.com

ISBN: 978-1-7336993-2-7 (paperback)
ISBN: 978-1-7336993-3-4 (ebook)

Library of Congress Control Number: 2023910130

Editor: Nicole Guenther
Illustration Designer, Art Director: Ifrah Fatima
Cover Art Design: Pawan Anjana
Creative Assistants: Achintya Thakur, Tan Tran, Airian Abad, and Lorenzo Daniels.

ATTENTION: WHOLESALE INQUIRIES
For more information on wholesale prices and discounts, please e-mail Satin Colorway Publishing Wholesale Department: inquiries@satincolorway.com

To my dear friend Kieran, for without you
I wouldn't be here to tell this story.

Cherries From A Thornbush, The Psychology of a Drowning Man, The Philosophy of a Drowning Man, The Structures Against Me, The Liability of Me, Woes of the Innocent Heart, The Flawlessness of Death... many names came to mind when choosing a title for the love of my life. These are some of the formers of this work, as they all were a perfect fit in their own way. However, not congruent with the art in their own right. It took months of allowing myself to feel all the emotions of regret, hopelessness, constant doubt, sorrow, pain, happiness, being left behind, and euphoria until I found the title that best represents this beautiful piece of art and my grapple with life during this time. I'm so incredibly terrified, but happy, to give you *Lavender is a Boring Color*.

LAVENDER is a Boring Color

Kevin Courtney Black

Satin Colorway Publishing

Here is the deconstructed thesis of my mind, heart, soul, and essence. Originally a passion project to find space for the overflowing thoughts of my existence.

I hope you cherish the spirit of all that I am. I hope you wield the thoughts and pain of me in love and tenderness. I hope, I hope, I hope...

preface

Sometimes I wondered,
how will I open this book?
A poetry book filled with my pain, my suffering,
my hope, my love, my connection to this vast universe,
my appreciation for the world,
and my plight with what we have constructed
of the world and the meaning of life.
For me, at this stage in my life - life is the social pillars
of the world that grasp my neck like a noose,
but there is no one to push me off the chair.

So I return to the question; do I start
such a piece of literature with...

Hi?

It feels so trivial to start with no weight in the introduction.
Nothing to bind the text with, or to show honor to.
I guess the better question would be,
why do I not value myself enough to introduce myself here?
Why do I feel as if I, as a person,
am not important enough to be introduced, especially
in my own writing?

I guess that's something I will have to work on.
Until then, I will say this;
welcome, welcome to the void that is in my heart
and the vision of which I feel as though I can no longer see.
This is not my story, for a story has an end,
and this is only my beginning. Enjoy.

midnight strawberries taste the best

PICKING SWEETNESS FROM A LEMON TREE

I want more days like this,
where the warmth from the summer nights with you
is as sweet as the ripened fruit on the vine.

So divine, I can taste your nectar by licking the remnants
of you off my lips.
What a treat that I may remember you in such a way,
I hope I always do.

As we fall into autumn
and float off the tree of euphoria,
I hope we are not separated.
I hope we glide into each other and intertwine as we ricochet
off the flow of us.
Can you do that for me?
Promise you'll never leave me,
and mean it.
Promise you won't hurt me and then never break my heart.
I trust you, I have trust in you, for you are too sweet
to ever be sour to me.
I hope I am as sweet to you.

THE GIFTS WE BRING

What a delight life is.
Why don't we appreciate her more?

We bring gifts for others.
For pain, we cry,
for death, we rest.
But for life?
We simply live it by running away from what truly matters:
Life herself and all the shimmers of light captured
in her sun-kissed beauty.

A REALLY BAD & ANNOYING POEM

My dearest,
I am sorry for how you found out
about my love for you.
I am sorry that you will never fully understand
why or how I came to feel this way about you.
Maybe it was your endless off-key singing,
or your frequent rants about stocks,
or perhaps your willingness to listen,
not just to me but to my heart.
Even when deaf,
you were always there to listen,
and even when I was blind, I couldn't take my eyes off you.
I loved you, I still do
and I'm so sorry that we couldn't be together,
even if we tried.

A DROUGHT IN TIME, SUNK THE SUN OF THE SKY

Time.
It moves with the pull of the tide,
the sinking of the sun,
and the rising of the moon.
Where'd all the time go?
Wasn't it here for me and you?

ORANGES ON A SUMMER NIGHT

Sometimes things fade,
and other times they are fading.
Life does both beautifully.
It's life's ultimate gift of art,
gracefully depleting while also creating life itself, anew.

Take the gift as a rebellious course of action,
it knows it can only exist within the confines of itself.
Thus, it slowly escapes to the love of its own artistic madness;

death. For she is beautiful.

THE TAUNT OF HAPPY

I always believed that home is where you're happiest.
Life happens at home because family happens at home.
Peace is at home because your space and place
in the world are wherever your home is.

Turns out, I was wrong.

NECTARINES ARE A CALIFORNIA FAVORITE

I assumed that everything in life would be perfect.
I also thought that a world where I could be happy, existed.
A world, where I would want to live, and never die.
But then you reminded me
that such a world only exists in the folds of my mind.
That the solid rock and metal around us is as warm as it gets,
in this cold world we call home.

A PHONE CALL AFTER DEATH

I'm so sorry the world couldn't give you
your own heart back.
Things _could_ have and _should_ have gone better.

The world doesn't have to be bitter,
love and happiness are true.
Therefore, I am so sorry,
that love and happiness couldn't find you.

Perhaps we were looking at it wrong;
life was never meant to be the end of pain,
for only death could bring such a beautiful offering.

DEVIL'S ADVOCATE

Have you ever considered that Life steps on you
not because it wants to, but because you're simply in the way
of where Life needs to step to move forward?

Why should life be blamed for your positionality?

THE FADED UNCHARTED TERRITORY /
/ THE BACKSEAT LOVER

I sit in the back. I am behind.
Quiet and unseen,
I'm stuck, trapped in a place that I do not want to be,
but I can't leave.
I love the presence of your trust
and the feeling of your warmth.
But underneath I'm cold, still cold.
You were supposed to be my blanket,
like the one you gave me.
Warm, soft, and always there for me, but I was wrong.

When the heart can't take the break anymore,
where do I run?
When the feelings inside bleed out and you're gone,
am I alone?
Some feelings hurt, some feelings don't,
and I get that but now I'm stuck in your backseat,
alone.

CHERRIES FROM A SEA OF CACTI

Turns out,
I can be shocked at how similar and different the world truly is
compared to how I imagined in my youth.
I am shocked at how vivid life can get when you allow yourself
to take the wheel that is being guided
by the light of your ancestors.
Could it be that I am genuinely shocked at how shocked I am not?
In all transparency, I am surprised at how understanding I am
of the medals and trophies for a life full
of disappointment;
happiness is a guise for everlasting suffering.

There are moments in life when you are happy,
but what happens when that happiness goes away?
Your emotions do not stop;
rather I came to realize, happiness is the misfire of our emotions.

Suffering, on the other hand, is ingrained in our biology.
We come into this world releasing our most sacred cargo,
our tears.
Conditionally we leave this world, the same.
Pockets of happiness do not signify a happy life,
yet pockets of sadness can feel like a lifetime of misery.
This is not wrong, because we are always suffering.

We overlook it trying to focus on the happy moments,
but the sad and excruciating moments are when we truly live.

PAIN

Pain.
Such a simple word,
it flows through my veins.
It reaps the benefits of eating my soul and stealing my leftover joy.
Channeling my ability to masquerade as a happy spirit
so that I may fall prey to my sorrow again.
It holds me, boundlessly grasping my heart.
Surrounding me,
yet making me feel alone.
Four little letters
to describe my constant ache.
Pain.

A BRUISED SOUL

I wish you would just hate me,
then it would be easier to get over you.
Instead, I'm here waiting,
like art on display; I'm a painting
bruised by the bristles of the paintbrush
that the painter can't see, because it's covered
in the palette that blends in with the sea.
Yet drowning in the painting is
me.

a quick break into crafting care:

come get your basket of warm misery,
fresh from the oven

CRAFTING CARE

What would it have been like?
Would I have woken up frightened,
or woken up familiar?
I wonder what he would have prescribed for me
if I would have left this flesh last night.

she nods her head

Well, I guess I'm forced to stick around
a bit longer.
Thanks for waiting for me again,
but I guess it wasn't time for me to go.
I wish I could say this is goodbye,
but we both know this is a *see you later*.

Hmm,
same time next month?
I might be free next week,
will tomorrow work for you?

TRIGGER WARNING

It's naïve to think that people care about you.
One day, sooner or later, we'll all be dead.
My time was just before yours.

                                        I wish I could be selfish,
                        then maybe someone would care about me.

UNDONE

It's unfortunate that the blood stains on the wall weren't enough
to make you care.
You're just like one of my *unconditional* loves,
how refreshing.
Caring about others only works
if you're at the center of it...

I thought I could believe in you.
I trusted you to care about me in a new way
and counted on you to understand:
me, we, and us.
I wear my scars on my shoulders so that you may be free
of implication.
All of this, just for you.

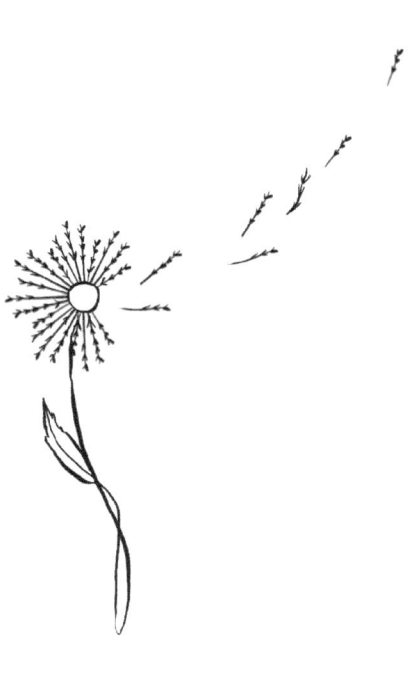

UNREALIZED FATE

I longed for eternity,
I never realized that time wasn't infinite.
I was chasing ideas of a distorted reality of endless love,
hoping we could stay and grow in that false society.
I thought we'd have forever
but your forever had an expiration date,
stamped with the approval from your heart and soul.

I wanted evermore, but you only cared for now.

Did you enjoy your crafting care break?
It was made just for you <3

Okay, back to telling you all about how these midnight strawberries taste the best.

SEIZING FALSENESS

I have been repeatedly told that life is
beautiful and that life is what you make of it
but if that were true,
I'd be happier.

JUICE BOX

Puncture me, crush me, and throw me away,
drained and confused.
The book closes, and the candle is blown out.
It's calm and dark,
Yet
the deafening sound of you trying to find me spikes my anxiety.
You want to hurt me; you are going to hurt me.

I hide while you seek.
The darkness has become my comfort.
Here I can be,
while here I am a book on the highest bookshelf,
chips on top of the refrigerator that you can't reach.
Why do you need me?
Isn't there something else,
someone else for you to squeeze the life out of?

You've found me;
please be gentle, I'm fragile.
You smile at me,
I look up and only see darkness,
as you stab me with no remorse.
What a cruel way to show that you love me.
What a cruel way to treat me, like I'm a juice box.

DOLLHOUSE

Am I not important to you anymore,
because I chose to exist?
Am I no longer enough for you,
just being me?
I thought I was your jewel, prized and valued.
Is a diamond no longer of value simply because it chooses not to
twinkle in the light?
Am I no longer your toy, just because I won't play along
with your perceptions of me?

I thought you liked oddities.
Isn't that why you chose me?
Because I wasn't like the others who were forged by the blades of
beauty, to be cut to perfection.

I guess you still haven't figured it out.
Too late, I'm done.
I will no longer play in your rotting dollhouse.

THE ROT OF A TOYED-WITH HEART

'Rotting' is a beautiful word when used in the context of me.
I am rotting slowly, yet quickly fading away.
Becoming anything but nice in appearance.
It hurts so bad.

Something's not right.
Who didn't take care of me?
Who brought me to this point of rot?
Is it fair to blame those around me when I already blame myself?
I can't take all the blame — there had to be signs.
Signs of neglect, signs that you were hurting me.
Not out of malice, but out of your own nature toward me.
I trusted you, I trusted all of you to be there for me,
to help me when I needed it and love me when I felt hopeless.

If only I knew then that I was asking for too much,
that my cries for help would be seen as over-exaggerations.
Then perhaps, this part of my story would end differently.

REALIZATIONS OF AN UNTETHERED GALAXY

I gasp for air,
but it is not there.

You are not there, you never are,
yet you are everywhere around me and in my heart.
You are me and I am you,
does that mean
I am alone?

THE PURPLE-DUSTED CONFLICT-OF-INTEREST: TEA FOR THOUGHT

I feel sick,
not unkept but ill in my soul.
Perhaps it's the feeling of pity in my heart?
I pity you,
seeping alone in your empty tea kettle.
I didn't mean for you to feel the weight of this existence.
I wanted you to feel my love pour in
and your hatred poured out.
Now look at us, both miserable.
When I touch your pot
your love no longer comes through.
Cool to the touch like the essence of you.

It was your cold heart
when all I needed was a warm hug.
Your inability to care for me
when all I wanted was your love.
Your careless talk
when all I wanted was peace of mind.

You brought me to this,
this pain, this doubt,
the stabbing feeling cutting through my skin,
you brought me blood,
but of course, it had to be my own.

You are the pain and misery I have.

It pains me to know
that I would be happy without you,
but sad with you.

THOUGHTS FROM A PUBLIC LIBRARY

Why must you make things personal?
Was it a noun? A person, place, or thing?
Or did an adjective set you off?
An action or occurrence?
Why does it matter to you?
Why did *that* situation set you off?

Dig deep, and deeper this time.

Uncover what has been hidden about yourself.
You may find beauty in the absolute horror of knowing.
Don't be afraid, lean into that feeling.
Life is naturally personal when you are the person;
that's the nature of life.

I don't know if I ever will understand
why you treat me like discarded plastic, damaging and a waste
of space.
I hope you find the answer
and that it haunts you until the end of your days.

THERE'S ENOUGH BLOOD FOR THE BOTH OF US

A friend once told me,
"Don't say you're sorry, 'cause I don't blame you."

She was right.
I don't blame you.
I'm not special, I'm not the diamond in the rough,
I'm just me,
ordinary, boring, nothing-special me.
It's times like this that I remember why you didn't look
at me the way I had hoped.
Why you continued to ignore me
when I was screaming for help.
The depth of the scars is all that mattered to you,
and mine was never deep enough for you.
No matter how much pain I was in,
no matter how much the tint of my reds mixed with the brown
of my skin
I knew you would never care.
But I cared for you so much
that, in my mind, I had enough care for the both of us.

CUPID'S KRYPTONITE

Actually, I am sorry,
I'm so sorry that you're incapable of caring for me.
I will always love 10 times harder and care 4,000 times more;
I guess that's the kryptonite of love.
Surrendering the lavenders of my peace
for the loveless shades of your disordered bleaks.

YOU, I

You are beautiful,
I am ugly.
You're the devil,
I'm the soul.
You hate,
I love.
You wait,
I go.
You stay,
I flow.
You,
I,
We
Are meaningless.

MISERABLE

He tried to love himself,
more and more every day;
breathing in acceptance,
exhaling anxiety.
He would reposition his love for others
as the love for himself.
Something she didn't want him to do.
For it was not that she actually loved him,
but rather,
it was the idea of him
that she loved.

Because she didn't love who he was, but
what he could be with her: miserable.

A SOMBER SKY OF AURORA LIGHTS

Sometimes I still think of her beauty in the clouds,
as dark and gloomy as she is, she's beautiful.
An artist of the sky, canvassing our bright star.
I can visualize every single raindrop fluttering
out of her, as it dances its way out of the sky, onto the earth.
Is she crying? Is she alright?
I turn to look for her face,
but through all that she is, it is hidden,
Never to be found or seen.

She's delicate, for now.
Stable, for now.
For even she knows she has the power of thunder and the strength of Zeus.
Rain rain, stay today, I do not want to see you go away.
It's *time* that she needs to heal with,
for it is graciously essential for her to cry,
so that she may feel her soul breathe again.

Through her likeness, I see a somber sky of aurora lights,
beautiful and yet so, so sad.

NOTHING

Inevitably, only nothingness can feel the room
when the air vanishes,
as the suffocation was supposed to be inescapable.

Yet here you are, dying in your own right — you're drowning.
What are you?

Dare I call you
human?

Or a brain that has lost touch with a life it once held?
Sorry, forgot.
They are each other's synonyms.

SOMETHING PAINFUL

Glass shatters,
flowers wilt,
the vase breaks,
and the mix of contaminated water and fresh reds of you blur,
all because the innocent got hurt.
How cliché.

Life is the verb of agony,
intricately making rainbows out of the mournful tears of the sky,
that we so thoughtlessly frolic in.

DON'T LEAVE

My thoughts are heavy,
mimicking the thick clouds of sawdust.
It's painful to breathe,
almost suffocating, but it only affects me.
Is my position too strong to be wielded?
Can I not move away?
No matter where I go the cloud follows me.
It knows me, and I am its home.
I know the cloud, it's familiar.
I'm safe through the endlessness of suffocation;
my gravity revolves around it,
just as it does me.
We're intertwined, two pieces of one double-tailed coin.

I think I'm afraid,
I'm afraid I will wake up to a fresh breath of air.
I'm afraid that once I do, the cloud will leave me.
Am I no longer worthy of the pain you inflict,
of the agonizing particles flowing through my lungs,
piercing my eyes, and cutting me off with each breath?
I thought the cloud was the source of my love,
my happiness,
the essence for which I am.
Life is beautiful when you can't see;
life is wonderful when I can't hear my own shouts of woe and
sorrow.

Somehow, I only know peace,
when it is positioned as the anguish of me.

INESCAPABILITY

Tears are daggers of lore,
we love affliction so much.
We secrete the one thing she loves the most, our passionate tears
of torment.
It can be quite enthralling for her that we desire to be free from her,
as she dances around our game of tug-of-war.
For she knows that we may never escape.

PLEASE FIND US IN ME AND OUR ALTERNATE UNIVERSE

Maybe he didn't care,
but she did.
She cared so much that she would kill herself,
if only to make him happy.
She'd rather hide her scars and smile,
so that he could do the same, just for a while.

PLEASE DON'T DO IT

Some advice?
Don't fall for me the way I fell for you,
don't show me the kindness
I sprung upon you.
It's not worth it;
my happiness rarely is.

So move on,
never talk to me again,
act like I don't exist,
and never let me cross your mind again.
It's safer this way for the both of us.

Life will move on.
Trust me, it always does.

I will miss you temporarily,
before the blur sets in any way.
Then you'll just be fragments
of the long-lost puzzle of my heart.

YOUR MIND CAN BE SO CRUEL FOR NO REASON

I can think of better things than marigolds and a peach rose,
for I truly believe the most beautiful things
are still foretold.

I'd rather dance with a hurricane
than hurt your soul.

The stars burn brighter knowing that you'll grow old.

Pretty brights in the sky
are just as nice
as the smile on your face
and the life in your eyes.

I know, you feel like crying and I'm so proud of you for fighting.
Hold on. Please. I beg, I know you are trying.

A SPOKEN WORD POEM

Why does the love I crave feel like treacherous waters?
Broad and full of the unforeseen,
constantly flowing into itself:
the unknown.

We don't know what's beneath the ocean,
and we may not know our own love,
but we know our own hearts.
The hearts that tell us to love,
the hearts that tell us to forgive,
just to hurt again.
The hearts that lie to themselves.

If we don't know our own hearts,
does that mean we don't know love?
Should I love without understanding my heart
or have a heart without understanding love?
Unknown and unforeseen,
love is like treacherous waters,

perilous, yet we call it beautiful.

A DISCONNECTED HYPOTHALAMUS

I don't hate you like you think I do,
but I am hurt, by a wound too deep to be forgiven
so soon.

I thought we had it.
We were supposed to be the two crafted to stand
the test of time.
It hurt to know that you never wanted such,
But no, I don't hate you and I'm not mad at you.
I'm just sorry I wasted so much time trying to be there,
for someone like you.

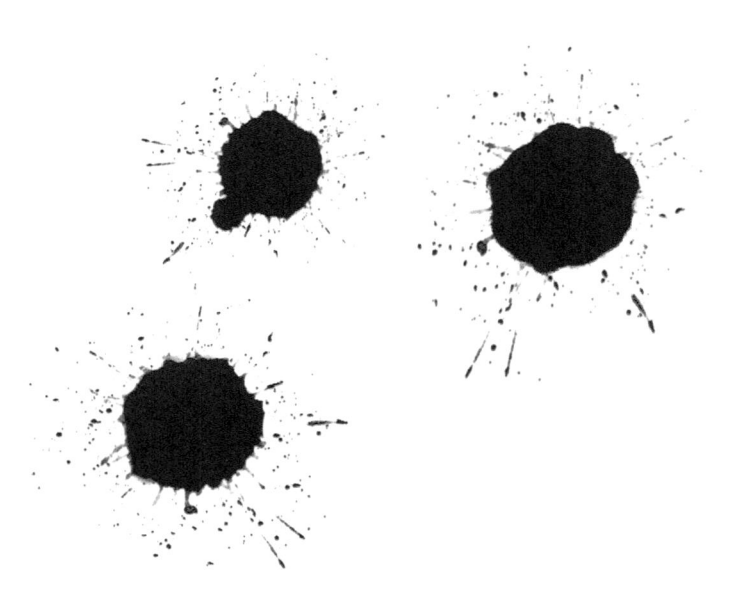

BLOTS ON A BLANK PAGE

He had to be sad
to know what true happiness felt like.
But in the end,
he had to give up his happiness
to know what her true sadness felt like, too.

LIFE, AN ACROSTIC POEM

Sadly, life is not always as light as the morning dew.
Ultimately, it is a gamble, the ultimate "all your eggs in one basket."
Indeed, life can be
Cruel but animated like a kid's whiteboard,
Illogical yet vivid. However,
Defining life is questioning death… and
Even the bravest of the brave cannot do that.

TRAUMA OF THE LAST TEAR

This is my last time apologizing to you,
You must know that I am sorry.

Sorry for not letting you in
when all you wanted was such.
Sorry for being quiet
when all you wanted was to talk.
When you needed the warmth of a hug,
I was cold and distant.
When you needed love,
I was detached and hard-hearted.
I wanted us to be happy, just like you wanted.
But the hatred in your heart,
outweighs the love in your soul.

For that, there is no cure.
For that, you and I,
our relationship is impure,
doomed from the start.
All because there is no room for love
in your heart.

You haven't discovered it yet,
and maybe you never will
but I am who I am.
My happiness is due,
and it's time for you to pay the bill.

A SOUL IS BORN

Suddenly a shift happened.
The dust in the room was spinning,
while the air in the room was thinning.
I thought the worst had come,
I thought the storm would end.

As the dust settled and the air came to,
I sat there in the rubble,
thinking, is this it?
Is this where I die before I am alive?
For what I had seen was inching toward me,
deadly and horrifying.
I look closely,
and see a wave of horror and sadness,
we call... life.

Is this life to be wielded,
if it can be so easily taken away?
Or to be protected with all our might,
if it is easy to break?

I can no longer feel my breath come in,
just as the absence of light ends.
The worst has finally come.
The wave of horror and sadness
is no longer near, it's here.
I open my eyes to see my new reality.

Welcome, welcome to a world
we call Earth.
Welcome to the beginning of your new end.

WILLINGLY GIVING YOU EVERYTHING

It hurts to open my eyes,
to see reality in the raw, and at face value.
It makes me feel ungrateful,
to not want to look at the world with the eyes that she gave me.
But I couldn't have imagined life to be this hard without you.
I look around and can't escape the delusion
that I still need to find a space for two,
a place for we.

But even the *we* was a mistake
fabricated by my mind so that my heart wouldn't be
wounded by self-mutilation.

It's the twist of a knife to say that I miss you
because I know you don't miss me.
Perhaps this is why I choose to not open my eyes.
They're safe closed, where darkness feels familiar,
like a friend that you openly confide your most sacred secrets with.

Goodbye to the unforgiving world around me,
I shall never see you again.
I close my eyes so that I may no longer think of we or you.
Finally, I am composed
and at peace.

interlude: the banana statement

I am allergic to bananas.

Please give me a banana,
preferably ripe, maybe with the tip near the stem turning speckled
brown, where someone might remark
maybe time to make banana bread soon.

gemini aesthetics

NASTY GREEN JUICE

You look beautiful here,
you look peaceful,
happy, even.
What changed?
Was it that someone believed in you?
aw, you poor waste of space,
I'm happy for you, truly.

They believed in you,
they loved you,
and they hated you for being you.
Congrats,
you're going to die alone,
because you couldn't just stop being yourself,
how tragic.

WINDOW VIEW

I enjoy that you're obsessed
with the fact that I'm not.
You don't like that I don't like you.
I thought you said I was obsessed?
That I needed to back up and fall back
like I was the maniac.

You had me fooled.
I thought I was crazy.
I cut you out of my life to get clean,
and now you're begging me to stay?

I love it,
you love the agony,
just as much as you hate
that you lust for me.
Your desires drive you insane,
making you fly across the deepest oceans
chasing the sun hoping I'd be there at the end of the finish line
waiting for you.
The fright of your desperation is maliciously misleading you.

What a joy
that I can see your heart throbbing,

are you scared?
Are you scared that you're the one who's really alone?

ADDICTION

I am honest, so I can tell you this:
the music you played was terrible,
but I didn't care.
You were my life jacket
when I was sinking into uncharted waters.

It felt hypnotic, the way I needed you in my life.
Like an addiction, without a remedy.

I was never enough for you,
I get that.

But you were always enough for me.
Enough to keep my heart beating and my hands sweaty.
So, I want you to remember
it was you who ruined us, not me.

I'M ALWAYS TRYING

Recently, I was confronted with a realization:
it's easier to laugh in the light
than cry because you were left in the darkness.

I would ride passenger in a life that was labeled mine,
with no controls given to me.
Questioning if being the passenger was the only way to be a part of your luminously
lifeless world.

You were the perfect amount to make me feel small.
As if the requirement to your heart was to breathe under a bathtub
of my most precious tears.

Forcing me to pull love and lust
from the cuts and bruises gifted by you.

ARLO'S RAINBOW

I have found that pain comes
from such a wonderful place,
the heart of your heart.

While hurt comes from the absence of care,
don't confuse the two.
One comes from a place of light
while the other is birthed
in the void of what and who was left behind.

THE COLD TOUCH OF ANEMIA /
/ THE WARM DRIZZLE OF SUN RAYS

Unfortunately,
the world is too much to hold in the grasp of me.
Sky too blue,
ocean too vast,
and space too limitless.

I am nothing but a man tainted by the figment of his imagination,
lured by the whimsical nature of self-indulging sorrow,
and burdened by the limitations of words to express my pain.
I paint a lavish world of life and yellow,
with a paintbrush of blue and black.

Do not fall for its tricks,
do not succumb to the draw and pull of the world I have painted.
It's the tribulations of my agony that make it enthralling,
not just the mask laced with deceit.

The glistening of my brown sun-kissed skin
constructs an image free of pain.
My toes dipped into a sea of bright eucalyptus green
and Atlantic blue,
for my fondness of nature and Poseidon.
Above is a rainbow arch of lavender, sage,
yellow, and orange behind a sky of the brightest blue.
Blissfully highlighting the light of life
and hiding the black canvas that it was painted upon.

Only my silence of what's unseen will bring the serenity matched in the painting.
My silence in the solitude of the clamor the world has sought after me.

AS COLORFUL AS A SPILLED MATCHA OATMILK LAVENDER LATTE

Sometimes, my thoughts would betroth me
before betraying me.
I would light a candle of wanderlust
that would encapsulate the aromas
that graced me when I felt alone. Quickly after
I would have a sweeping wave of depression.
It was a familiarly delightful combo, that left me wishing
that I would soon take my last exhale.
As I would cry, the ideas fluttered around
in my head like a beautiful butterfly garden.
Colorful and exhilarating,
clustered and unable to breathe.

I would seek and long for it all to stop.
Stop the pain of being alone and the feeling
that something was wrong with me.

Oh *mercy*, why have you left me?

Can I not pull myself up out of my own misery,
a bystander in my own life, tagging along
in a vessel of flesh until my death?

Hey, may I ask a question?
Is it still considered holding my thoughts in,
if I force them to bleed out until I feel something again?

LESSONS FROM INSIDE A GLASS JAR

I can see you, can you see me?
I hope you can, you're looking at me.

Through all the particles of green and everything
that's filled with uncertainty,
I'm here — and you know that.
Please, drink up, so that you may see me more.
Please, look deep into the glass jar,
I should be there.
Trapped between the existence of life and the dust
of the thick abyss that surrounds me.
Please see me, I am not lost,
But I am stuck in self-inflicted solitary.

I am trapped, yet I am told that I am free.

But don't be fooled, although I see everything,
the double glass barriers still surround me from all sides; mirroring
the environment for the view of others but transparent
for me.

As you come closer, you do not look for me.
You look for yourself and see what you want to see.
How charismatic,
how charming.

DE LA LUNE ET VOUS
(LE TROISIÈME // THE 3RD)

What's done is done.
You were right next to me, and yet you didn't notice.
You walked past me like I was nobody,
I wanted to be there for you,
but you wanted me nowhere near.

I'm taken back, hand on my heart repulsed and at a loss for words.

I thought you actually loved me.

I guess I was wrong.
She's your sun,
but I was your moon.

I just hoped I would always be around you.

DE LA LUNE ET VOUS
(LA DEUXIÈME // THE 2ND)

Forget it,
forget what I said,
I do know the difference,
I do know what makes me and you.
(sigh)
You are the difference,
you are the one I call out to at night
when I feel hopeless and helpless.
You are the one I care for and care about,
no matter the distance.
You are there for me and I am there for you,
even when your head is pounding, breathing feeling thin,
and you long for that sweet release of your nighttime medicine.
I look at your face and see your strength and perseverance.
For even when I can't see you,
I know that my heart wants to tell you,

I love you,
my dear lune.

DE LA LUNE ET VOUS

There can't be a you and me
without love.
The love between you and me
travels to Jupiter and back every night,
desperately waiting for the moment when Pluto may intercept our
play of love,
so that we may go further out together,
without pain or worry.

I hope and pray that the stars are on our side,
for then the earth could never keep us away.
My heart feels stuck, waiting for the stream of your love to canvas my
lips again.
I can't help but to blush
over the lavender-laced daydream of your cheeks rosing over me.

I wonder if you think of me, the same way I giggle
when I profoundly hallucinate about you.

Dear my sweet sweet love,
will you leave me so that I may miss you?
Leave me so that I can want to cherish you,
but never depart from me
so that I may always be with you.

I love you, I love you, I love you, my dear lune.

A DOVE IN THE MIND OF MY HEART

So now, I must ask you.
Would you love me if I changed?
If I stopped being me?

If you could truly see the seeds of lavender that I have sowed,
and happiness that I have planted and forged come true to the eye,
would you look at me differently?
Even a little?
Knowing all my past is now lost
now that I have unbounded myself from a predetermined future
and untethered myself from the path I was once walking upon.

Or maybe you would hate me?
Not for changing,
But for changing without my heart's consent. I did this
for you, and yet pushing myself out
of my comfort zone, removing my own boundaries,
and letting people in when I didn't know that I could — gave me more pain
than I could ever self-inflict.
I had to pay the price for an ungodly change that my heart and eyes did not want.
So that one day you may look upon me
with the sun-kissed remarks of love and desire in your eyes.

So I ask again:
Will you hold me?

Will you have me?
Will you take me?
If not for love,
or the changes I have made,
for my cowardly heart that is too afraid to lose you,
and yet terrified, still changed for you.
Please, I must know,
will you love me if I change?

HOME

Some of my favorite things happen at home;
love, lust, and the cool breeze from my bedroom fan on a hot humid day.

It's the only place I can sit around all day
and still say I had a good day.
Within these four walls,
I'm a monarch to the kingdom with the most vast resource,
my imagination.

HOME (ALTERNATIVE)

You must understand, home isn't a place.
Places close, crumble,
get ransacked,
demolished, and degrade over time.

You are my home, what I look forward to after a long day at work.
Accepting of my comfort, my safe haven.
.
Look towards home when you feel like giving up,
and heal in it when you are hurt.

Most importantly, protect it like you are the last person
standing against its destruction,
like if that food in your refrigerator you were craving all day
was about to be eaten by someone else without the consent
of your tastebuds.

Remember, you may never leave home.
Take it, change it, or build it up,
but never get rid of it.

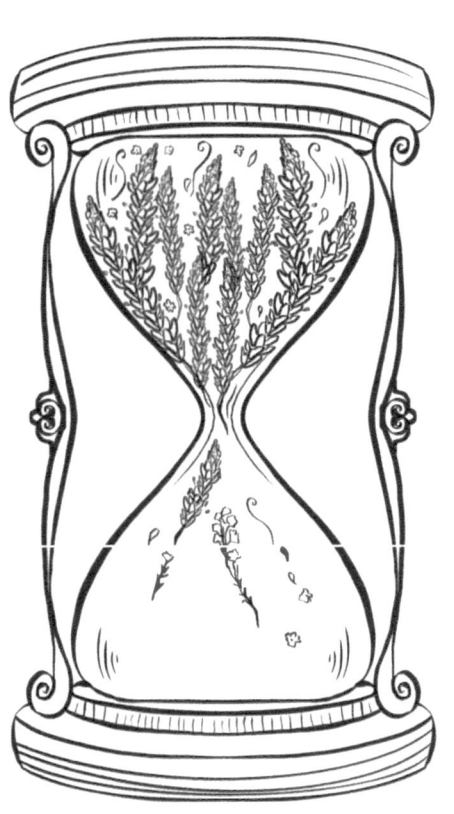

HOURGLASS: FREE

Life felt inconsequential without you.
I felt lost and exposed.

Thankfully, I learned
you must drain the swamp that suffocates you,
to be free of the water that torments you.
I'm free now,
my side of the hourglass is empty,
I no longer want you. I returned your gift of suffering,
because like the contents permit in an hourglass,
only one of us can truly be free.

HOURGLASS: TORMENT

Stop.
Do not allow yourself to wallow,
don't give them the satisfaction,
as drowning is the ricochet of torment,
and the consequence of guilt.
It was never my responsibility to make you feel happy,
I wanted you to be happy, but it's not my fault you weren't.

Refuse it,
do not be enthralled by the bag of warm fresh
guilt they have baked for you out of their oven of self-hatred.

Do not give them the pleasure of your misery.
You are better than that,
so act like it.

CHANGES IN TERMS AND CONDITIONS

I wonder if the sky is still blue,
if the birds still chirp, if the seeds
of lavender still bloom, and if the water
still sparkles in the moon light.
The callouses on our hands are a testament
to no matter how much we try to claw
our way out, no matter how many tears
of frustration and longing
for someone else to come save us
from our own minds occur,
we are still here — wallowing and abandoned,
left to sink in this hole of no escape and dirt.

How did we get here?
How did we become consumed with hopelessness?

I don't know why we cannot escape
or how long we've been falling in and out
of love.
While being dragged down this purgatory of damnation
as if we spoke in blasphemy
for the reason
we were pushed down here in the first place,
bound together only to suffer.

CHANGES IN TERMS AND CONDITIONS (CONTINUED)

I see you, and the light that we once graced.
You may never forgive me
for something I didn't do.
That something being the direct cause of your insanity
and outrageous imagination.

To this, I am sorry, and for this,
I must let you go.
I must allow you to flourish without me
and your rancid mind.

I owe it to the world to let you breathe
in the fresh air that feels so new,
without me tied to you.

I owe myself much more for getting us out,
so go ahead, breathe.
We are now without eternity and without a we.

Deep breaths,
deep breaths.

NOISES OF THE PASSING

A whistle in the wind can be carried for miles,
thinning as the free flow drifts.

The pure sound of the air
circulates around the birds traveling in it,
piques the curiosity of the hollowing uproar of the mountains,
and dances upon the ears of the Deaf.

The whistling silence
deafens the pandemonium of the world,
and leaves nothing but a soul ripe with dwindled clatter.

GALAXIES AWAY

The stars look so faint from my view,
even the solar particles of such stellar could no longer be felt
with my inhale.

They were dimming by the minute, I heard.
Losing essence by the second, I was unwillingly reassured.

The universe is already such a dark space.
I see that we often like to resemble it within our galaxies
beneath our skin.

We constantly drift and pull away from ourselves.
It's familiar, comforting as we find solace
in the endless cold that we unknowingly long for.

Perhaps it was never about what my universe wanted,
but what it meant to bloom the death of me
for the abundance of the galaxies.
Ah, now I see.

THE DEATH OF A PURE SOUL

I'd rather drown than feel my feelings bleed out of my chest,
screaming in angst that I am not in control.
I no longer can see a future that was pressed upon me
by the structures against.

Against: my happiness.
Pro: my sorrow.
Against: my rest and sleep.
Pro: my tears and suffering.

All I want is to prosper.

I heard prosperity comes with peace.
Peace is acquired when Zen is achieved,
and Zen is only achieved when you are in control.

Notice how I have to go backward to go forward.
These are the structures I speak of,
the beams of my dread and fear,
the power that I do not hold because I was looted of free will.
The will to smile, the will to a warm hug that makes everything right,
the will to have my own comfort in the presence of discomfort, the
will of me.
I speak to you again, please understand
that these are the structures against me.

THE CRY THAT WASN'T HEARD

Hmm...
I've realized now that no matter what I do,
I ruin you, break you down, and burn you.
Fragile, like the sound of our robust atmosphere
ripping through wind chimes.
It sounds familiar, like the clatter of devastation
when you realize that you aren't enough.

I did this, I have to live with it,
and for that, I am so sorry, body.
I am so sorry that I keep putting you through
the constant pain and heartbreak
of trying to be better for them, and not for us.

If one thing is to be true then I must finally show you
my colors of true black and blues.
I want you to know that I love you,
and hope that one day,
without help,
without crying and the feeling of loss,
we can be happy.

At last, I see the vision.
At last, I see that I need to stop hurting me,
at last, at last, at last,
I hope to do better,
for me.

ACCEPTING A BLIND MULE

Acceptance is unnatural.
Why would you seek approval for your own will?
Remember, the heavens are not here on Earth,
but disapproval is.
People will disapprove of you,
your life,
your happiness,
and your peace.
That's natural.
If there is anything that you need
to seek approval for
it is the acceptance of disapproval
as that is the embodiment of life.

FORGIVENESS

I hope that one day you can forgive me.
Maybe we will look back at today when we bump into each other
at our favorite garden near the bay
and awkwardly catch up with nothing real to say.

As we gaze back at how much we needed to grow for us to be happy,
we admire how much we have sprouted separately.

I hope a day like this comes to fruition,
a day where I can finally forgive you
for all the disgusting words you have gifted me.
A day of forgiveness.

HATE

I hate that you hate me.
You don't know that you hate me,
but you do.
You hate everything that I am,
and hate everything I will become (me).
A tattoo-having, iced oat milk lavender matcha drinking,
dance anywhere music is playing, and truly accepting of all walks
of life type person.
Your cold existence in my life only feels fulfilling for you
since it gives you your self-peace.
You love the pain I have,
because it makes you feel happy.
I hate that you hate me,
but you love to hate.

JEANS IN THE SUN ~ COLOR VISION

The great elephant knows all,
sees all, understands all,
yet holds no one.

It is a symbol, a beacon,
jumping around the darkness of our minds,
lighting up the spaces between and about.
Oh, how the natural hues of gray and white
have never been so bright.

It's as if I can sit and pray for a better day,
a day of peace,
where I may lay down
under the gray tree, in the bright gray grass.
and wait in my jeans
for the luminous gray sun to pass;
then, and only then, will I ever see peace.

AUGUST 4, 2021

I've come to learn that
life likes to be funny and spontaneous.
Nothing in the world can prepare you
for the silliness of life
and the clownery but intentionality
of the universe.
To be ready,
you must simply have no expectations.

I realize now that my interpretation of life,
is based on my perception that
things happen because they have to.
While I still believe I am right,
I know I am also wrong.

Life happens because you deserve the delicacy of breath
not the ruthlessness of fate.

CREATIVE // DIFFERENCES

I'm too distant from those I need to be close to,
and too close to those I need to be distant from.
I need to be intentional of who I put around me
and who I let in.

Through the fog of a rainy day,
I only see myself drowning in the water droplets
of my misinterpretations.
The haze of all that made me great
is in the fabric of chaos I call
the deconstruction of my mind.

DIFFERENCES // CREATIVE

I want to be better, I need to be me.
Not the false narrative that parades around in my head
pretending to be me.

Was it my delusions that brought my soul
to the point of fracture?
My curiosities that broke the dam keeping me at bay?

Clarity has never been my friend,
but has always been the ally of my doubt,
and the foe of my vision.

I hope through the questioning trials
of my accomplishments,
I will still find what I've been looking for:

the quietude of a mind fraught with internal war.

FROWZY HOPE

Truthfully,
there are moments in my life,
I wonder:
what's next?

Is this the peak of my existence,
the purpose of my soul?
Even when I feel like I could be so much more,
I feel so much less.

The book closes,
The chapters move on,
and I'm stuck.
I'm stuck in the beginning but somehow left behind
in the spine of my own book of life.

I feel misplaced,
like a bookmark
without a bookcase.
Although I feel astray,
I look ahead and forward,
for these little moments
are why I am here
suddenly and blindly enjoying life and all of her offerings.

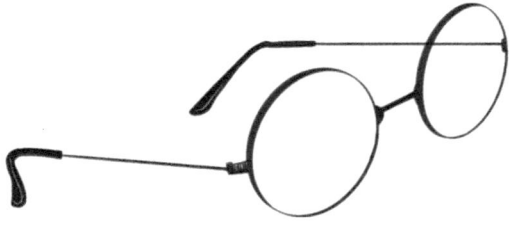

OPTIMISM'S BLIND EYE

Life can feel like a whirlwind,
spinning through the fabrics of time
bringing us closer to who we want to be.

In the eye of the storm,
there is no exit, no clear direction,
and in a moment's notice, you're plopped into
an abyss of what is and what was.

We must be optimistic,
decisive, and live with intentionality.
For only then,
will we see the light,
in the eye of the storm we call life.

TIME MACHINE

- I ~~hope~~... *no too wishful...*
- I ~~know~~... *too confident...*

Life works out, I think.
For some, I feel that it's supposed to be hard, unbearable even.
But when the moment comes
where everything falls into place,
life — real life — happens.
And when it does,
you may never go back.

Time is a weird concept
filled with such life
and wrapped with misfortune, wisdom, and mayhem.

Life and all of her adversaries are a cohort
like I've never seen before.

Stories untold,
fabrics of time ripped and throttled,
secrets that will never be unraveled,
and yet, here we are,
living in the present
and the past in perfect harmony.
We live most of our lives trapped in the past,
and our entire life chasing the future.

Time is not real.
Life is, so enjoy every second of it.
And maybe,
just maybe,
you will feel her bliss.

PERFECT ADJACENT

Some days are just perfect.
We don't know it until it happens,
but perfection is crafted, never given.
Such perfect days are molded from the purest crystals
rife with happiness.

Sometimes, it may be hard to see
such crystals in the presence of the dark clouds within
the deep fog of our minds.
But they are there,
waiting for us to find them.

On our journey through life, remember,
perfection is never truly perfect.
Even through the days of radiance
and the citrusy warmth of oranges,
there will always be a more perfect day,
eagerly awaiting your arrival.

A SHREDDER IN THE BLACK HOLE OF MY MIND

The shoe fits,
the clock ticks
the book has spoken,
another door opens.

I breathe.
For a second, all is well.
For a second I fabricate the illusion that I am at bliss,
because I have inner peace and home in my heart,
love in my arteries,
soul in my mind,
and thought in my body.

Why would I wish to seek a world that does not exist?
Why would I create deceitful imageries of peace
when we are always at war with ourselves and one another?
I know I have been alive for a very short amount of time
with respect to the wide and vast universe that contains the spectacle
of our planets as they whirl around our sun
in a string of celebration until their
lights become nothing but a flicker,
but somehow I do feel hope.

I cannot define or describe it,
but it's there,
prancing around the essence of my being,
in a prayer circle.

That's my hope, our hope.
We must never lose it, for if we do,
we may only fear the one who found it instead.

RIGORS OF HOPE

No matter how callous,
or steep,
the world knows the evitable.
That's how it sustains us.
Life is pure knowledge,
you must learn to enjoy it.

Before we're taught to laugh,
we're born in this world distraught and crying,
and we often leave it the same.
Life is fascinating,
truly God's best work of art,
as complicated and careless as it may feel,
life is intentional in all it does,
and all it has to offer.
From the lightness of a lotus flower
to the depth of the pond it drifts upon,
everything is calculated. So please,
if not for me — for you,
enjoy every moment,

I know I will,
won't you?

THE FLOWER THAT BLOOMED

Why does a child draw a flower?
Is it for the thrill of coloring in the petals,
or the swiftness and simplicity of drawing the stem?

Can the child not just be happy and enjoy the drawing?

The dissection of the smallest things is human nature;
we dissect our world to fill our corrupt minds,
as if beauty isn't in the art of just doing.

Even a child knows that bliss
is something you cannot achieve by asking,
but only in a state of being.

THE FLOWER THAT BLOOMED, INTERLUDE: INTERPRETATION'S WHIM

The blues and reds are the meanings of us,
carelessly vibrant,
but oh so dull.

THE FLOWER THAT BLOOMED (PART 2)

The child paints the stems and petals
of the blooming flower to show the color and range
illustrating the vibrancy of life and all its essence.
For us it is the peace in knowing that something so delicate
and dainty,
could be a source of simple joy across nations,
wars, and unrest.
What is it about the gleaming of the sun that offers
the colorways of life to extend beyond such green stems?

We must see beyond what our minds can fathom,
for in front of our irises and pupils is a world known and familiar,
but behind the box
that our imagination is trapped in
is a world of unknown and wonder.
Seek to wonder, not to examine,
seek to see life as life, not a philosophical question,
seek the flower.

GIVING UP CONTROL

The withering of peonies and the blooming of chrysanthemums
is my favorite season.
The peonies change from reflective pink petals to the demised droop
of a once colorful life.
A time fraught with weather that's not too hot, not too cold,
transitional, but oh so bold.

The beauty of nature
has to die for the next wave of life to flourish.
The exchange of endless beauty
is harrowing like the jump into a new relationship,
but necessary, like knowing when you outgrew the one before it.
Symbolizing the passage of time,
and the honor and pity of age.
What a change,
what excite.

interlude: opening-up

I'm tired of writing about the same old stuff, over and over again.
Everyone writes about darkness and sadness;
like, we get it,
poets are depressed.

the revival of a collapsed sun

THE LAST HURRAH

Poetry is a form of art;
make one bad move and everyone hates it.
It goes down the drain,
out the window,
in the garbage,
then seen in the trash,
and hated all over again.
Is it bad art, that I should call it?
Or is it poetry, as I once knew it?
I'd rather die a bad poet
than someone who used to be a crafting tool to a dying art piece.
Poetry is living,
breathing, and moving.
For that is real poetry:
raw,
untouched,
unfathomable,
thought-provoking, yet simplistic,
dashing yet captivating and undone.

It should close by making you feel something,
whether it was made in the whim of a hasty deadline
or in the moment of happiness
where you remembered the value of your own life;
it is the unknown about the upbringing of the piece,
that makes poetry
misunderstood.

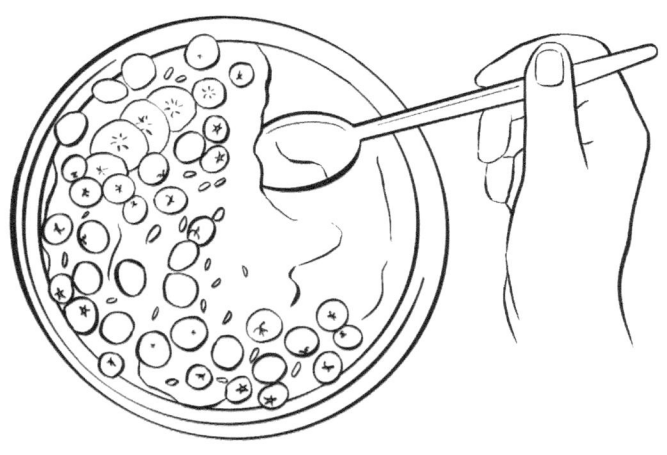

BLUEBERRIES IN MY AÇAÍ BOWL

I always believed that perfection
was too perfect to obtain.

Then you showed up,
perfectly perfect in your hue of blue,
in your pool of pigmented purple.
To me, this is the color of love,
to me, you are fascinatingly succulent
and lusciously colorful.
Rounded out by the fruits of your will,
you are a Goddess,
sprouted from the roots of those before you.

I hope I cherish you,
and I hope you nurture me.
For in this universe,
we were meant to live in such abundance.
My perfect blue, may our time together
simply be.

EYE OF ABUNDANCE

What is abundant happiness?
Is it the core feeling of light
or the plant that grows in the dark at night?
Only my eyes can tell my abundance of light,
so only I can see the happiness within me.

INNER THOUGHTS OF WAR

Do you love yourself?

Do you even know what love feels like?
Has anyone ever shown you unconditional love?
The kind that breaks boundaries,
is transparent through the thickest
of fogs, and is a beacon of light in the hell
of our own minds?

The world is beyond too cruel,
for you not to show yourself love.
I hope you can learn what love is.
Like a child when they get their first friend
or the indulging of your favorite ice cream
after a week of that diet, you knew you couldn't keep.
I was once told the feeling of love is like you are being
grounded to earth but bound to the heart.

I want you to know what it truly feels like
when you know you are loved. I pray that you already do.

So, I ask you again:
do you love yourself?

I ALREADY MISS YOU

This is it,
this is life,
one forged in suffering and ravaged by the world.
Simply to be drowning in air,
falling into a cup,
and being electrocuted by a shoe.
I hate life, it doesn't make sense
like swimming in a lightbulb,
it's electrifyingly excruciating,

I hate it
I hate it
I love it

I love the feeling of thrill,
the uncertainty of winning,
the warmth of that one person
you can eat a bowl of gummy bears with
and never get sick of them.

CLARITY

Now what do I do with this 20/20 vision?
I've never seen anything as clear,
even with the glasses I have, I've been blind.
Can I tell you a secret?
It was never about you,
It has always been about me and my journey to self-love.
I see that now.
I see how I projected my lust for self-love onto you
as if you were a blank canvas that I needed to paint.

I'm sorry but grateful.

Because of me, I see myself.
I see that I project at an astronomical level.
I see that I need to gain the object permanence
required to understand my own self-love.
It's there, it's always been there, but I acted as if it came from others
as if I needed you there to fill the void.
But now I realize, I was the void of my own void.

I have decided that I do love myself
and that I can't see anybody else loving me better than me.

SOMETHING POSITIVE

Be reassuringly positive in all that you do.
So that one day you may look up, and see how beautiful
the world is that crafted the wonders of you
in the likeness of fortitude.

You may be cheerful so as not to stifle what's within.
But you can also be real with yourself.
Breathe and feel the emotions of gratitude for your past
self that positioned you where you stand now.
For even in the light, there are grains of which no spectacle can see,
as the future is a mirage.

So I invite you:
flourish in your fountain of youth,
bloom like a blooming tea,
be predictably unexpected,
and look for admiration within,
as that is when your true self begins.

PHILOSOPHY IS A LOSING GAME

Bask in all that Gaia has to offer us.
I want you to pay attention to this question:

If the sun is the symbol of eternal life,
is that why we like to gaze upon the moon?
For even when reaching for the stars,
we limit ourselves to the bounds of our imagination.

I would like to say that it is the light of a candle,
that calms the mind and brings the body serenity.
But it is not.

It is the steadiness of the open flame and the sight
of the slow demise of the aromatic wax,
that keeps the human at bay.

For it is never what the mind truly seeks,
that surprises us the most, and we ought to seek the surprise.

Explore the already known about yourself,
did you miss something hiding beneath the surface?
Or investigate the part of you
that is scared to see beyond
what you already realized about yourself.
See, life can be quite wonderful
when you know how you want to live it.

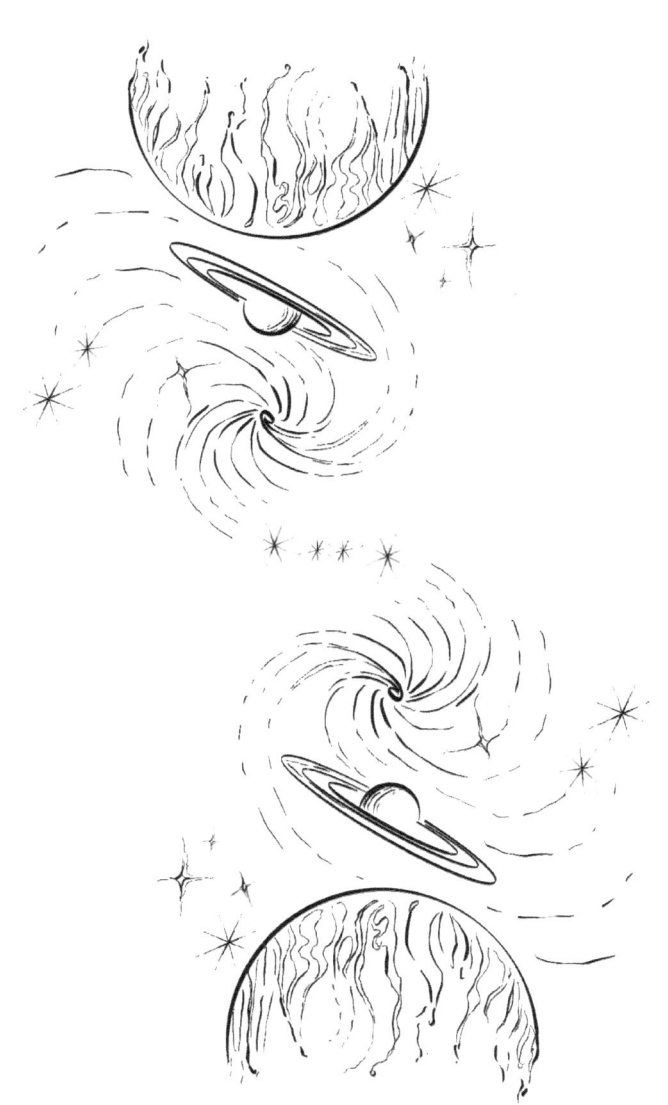

THE COSMOS

A rainbow is mere fragments of light,
dancing around the great blue.
For a moment it's beautiful,
for a moment it is real,
but by the second,
it is gone.
That's how I describe the beauty of life,
forever fading into the oblivion of nullity,
like the last breath of a fleeting laughter
that was once heard for miles.

A UNIVERSE OF LOVE

As even the sun has to go away
so that the moon may dance with the stars in the sky,
and gaze out into the galaxy that beholds them.

Beauty has never been far away
when the love of the cosmos has always been here to stay.

AFRO

Hydration is key;
you need to hydrate,
so that the world may see the beauty of it all,
so that the sun compliments and
dances in the background in celebration,
so that the crown may not tilt
and stand righteously powerful and protected by its own might.

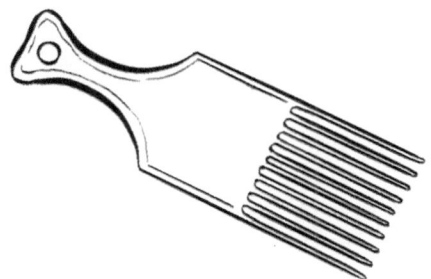

Oh, the beauty,
oh, the power.
Glistening in all the light mother earth has to offer,
you truly are perfect;
thank you for choosing me.

PERFECT ADJACENT (REPRISE)

Some days are just perfect,
golden in the sunbeams,
and beautifully crafted.
They are the expression of light
and the manifestation of our dreams.

But to have a truly perfect day,
we must acknowledge how an imperfect day feels.
Perhaps the feeling of seeing a smoky burnt toast
pop out of the toaster
after salivating over it all morning,
or stubbing your toe rushing out the door hoping to not be late again,
yet knowing you will be.

It's okay to accept that
life herself does not need to be perfect;
that's what makes the perfect days, perfection.

THE TRIPLE VISION AS FORESEEN BY THE COSMOS

Who knew that the lavender and blues of your heart
would be the boring colors of our art.
Swished and sloshed around like the fading hues of our passions,
coupled with the misalignment of your brain that faded away
simply because there was rain.

Do you ever doubt your mind?
Doubt that you are supposed to be here
and that this is the purpose of your life?
Our lavenders often feel meaningless until the blues
of our auras intertwine into something beautiful, *us*.
.

Is it possible that only our lavender is unique,
So that our blues may be the brunt of us?

I won't stop running, looking for our colorful wanderlust,
as my mind gets lost and our colors become more robust.
For even rainbows can't be untethered,
so I ask, may we be freed
of our tortured lavender and blues forever?

SUN ROSE

A quintessential perfect sun rose can be forged
in the flames of the coldest sea of eucalyptus.
Fresh and fragrant,
but competing for warmth and love.

I asked you once if you'd care about me forever;
forever doesn't end when the last rose petal has fallen,
nor does it end when the rays of the eternal flame
stop and the night sky befalls us.

Think back to when we were we,
rooted in the dirt that made us flourish
in the grounds of our own care.
Was it worth it? The end of an era
so that you can feel like the big stalk,
the one that was picked
because perfection is too beautiful to just be.

I see it now, through the thick façade.
I don't need you,
but you need me,
you need the grace of my heart to care
for the emptiness of your life.
The compassion of my tea-making when you're sick,
and the bread we break in the sun when you win.
All of this for you while you hope I bask in your shadow.

Do you feel it? Feel the pressure that I put back on to you.
It's damaging,
unequivocally ravaging the fields of your joy.

LAVENDER IS A HEAVENLY COLOR

It has always been my first love.
The warm sweet aroma on a flowery sunny day,
the bees gathered around it in the spirit of giving,
and the glowing nectar that oozes from its beauty.

Ah,
I can still smell it even on
winter days like this.

I'm sorry that I called you insignificant,
cast you away, and made you feel unimportant.
It was the sin of looking for myself
in others
that caused me to be so careless.
You are bright and radiant in the likeness of the sun.
Forever alluring and never boring,
I hope you accept my apology.

I will put my needs and desires first,
and that includes you,

my
lovely fragrant and whimsical
lavender.

www.ingramcontent.com/pod-product-compliance
Lightning Source LLC
Chambersburg PA
CBHW060354080526
44583CB00012B/308